Spilling the beans...

MAKING IT IN

FOOTBALL

First published in 2001 by Miles Kelly Publishing,
Bardfield Centre, Great Bardfield, Essex CM7 4SL

Printed in Italy

ISBN 1-84236-009-4

24681097531

Cover design and illustration: Inc
Layout design: Mackerel

The author would like to thank Paul Konchesky and
everyone at Charlton Athletic Football Club.

Spilling the Beans on...
MAKING IT IN
FOOTBALL

by Matt Parselle

Illustrations   Martin Remphry

Miles Kelly PUBLISHING

Titles in the Series:
Making it in Football
Making it in Music
Making it in the Movies
Making it in the Ballet
Making it in the Fashion Industry
Making it in Computers

Contents

This book is dedicated to the memory of
Jack Parselle 1942-1999

About the Author

Matt Parselle is a full-time football journalist. He contributes articles on the game to websites and a number of magazines and part-works. This is his first book about football. He lives in south London and is a season ticket holder at Charlton Athletic.

Introduction

Hands up if you've ever done any of the following things:

a given a running commentary on yourself, John Motson-style, whilst playing football with your mates down the park ("...Beckham beats one man, then another, this is a fantastic run by David Beckham but what will he do next?... Oh, what an incredible goal!!!").

b found yourself glued to the television on Saturday afternoon, watching the teletext football pages roll over and over as you keep an eye out for any updates to the scores.

c practised your signature over and over whilst fondly imagining hordes of screaming fans begging you to autograph matchday programmes/bits of paper/bits of their bodies.

d solved the dilemma of wanting to watch two different matches which are on at the same time on different channels by getting hold of two tellies and placing them side-by-side in the lounge.

If your hand shot up to one or more of the above questions then the chances are that you're in love with *The Beautiful Game*. You are a football fan. Don't panic though, you're not alone. In fact, by following football, you actually have something in common with an awful lot of people. How many exactly? Well, after a great deal of research, we're still not sure, but believe us, it's quite a lot – millions, maybe even billions.

And we're not going to go into the reasons why football is such a great game here, either. Why? Because that would take another whole book in itself!

The point is, a huge number of people across the planet watch and enjoy football. And, at times, a large number of them have no doubt dreamed about playing the game at the highest level (you included if you put your hand up to a or c), whether it be lifting the FA Cup as captain of their team in front of thousands of adoring fans, or scoring the extra-time golden goal winner in the World Cup Final. But only a tiny fraction of those people actually play football and, this is the important bit, get paid for it.

For example, in England there are roughly 600 players in the Premiership. When you consider that England has a population of around 60 million, the odds on making it to the top don't look that good.

But all is not lost. If you decide that a life in football is for you – and let's face it, who wouldn't want to make a living by playing their favourite game – then help is at hand ... in the shape of this book. Obviously we can't make you as skilful as Zinedine Zidane or as famous as Michael Owen, but we might be able to point you in the right direction. And hopefully, you might also find out a bit more about what it takes to be a top footballer. By the end you should know everything you'll need to know about the wonderful world of football.

Dream Team

Let's imagine for a moment that you're in your early twenties – 23, say. You are a professional footballer playing for one of the top sides in the country, and one of the best clubs in Europe. Every week you turn out in front of huge crowds who love you and chant your name. Not a season goes by without you and your team winning at least one major trophy. Your one great worry in life is which of your five sports cars you will roll up at the training ground in. You have a gorgeous model girlfriend and you're incredibly handsome with a very nice haircut. Oh, and you earn around £50,000 a week. Not including win bonuses and multimillion pound payouts for wearing a particular brand of football boots.

Sounds all right, doesn't it? Certainly better than frying burgers for £3.50 an hour and it's no wonder that so many people idle away the hours dreaming of such a glamorous life. You

probably have too, or you wouldn't be reading this book.

However, there is a catch. In fact, there are quite a few. Indeed it's fairly unlikely, even if you do play in the Premiership, that your day-to-day existence will be quite as happy-go-lucky as the one described above.

It sounds obvious, but not everyone who is a professional footballer gets to play for Manchester United or Liverpool. Or Arsenal, or whichever club you imagine covering yourself in glory at. Don't forget, there are three other divisions (not including non-League teams), and most footballers will play for a number of clubs during their careers. Clubs which may include the likes of Grimsby Town and Hull City.

And, of course, there's nothing wrong with that. You can still earn a decent amount of money and enjoy a successful career, at such clubs. But it's unlikely you'll be turning up for training every morning in a chauffeur-driven Ferrari F355 with personalised number plates and a PlayStation built into the back seat. In fact, you're more likely to have to hitch a lift with a few team-mates as you make your way to the ground through the wind and the pouring rain.

Ah yes, the weather. In your dreams of World Cup-winning glory, you probably pictured a beautiful pitch, in a stunning hi-tech stadium, on a fantastic sunny day with barely a cloud in the sky. Sadly, football is not by and large (unless you actually *are* playing in the World Cup) a summer sport. The season lasts from August to May and you're likely to encounter a wide variety of weather.

And whatever the weather is – rain, snow, hail, even blistering heat – you still have to turn up every day at some wind-swept field known as the training ground. Then exercise your socks off for the next  few hours while a red-faced coach bellows orders at you. Anyone who doesn't enjoy cross-country runs at school in the freezing cold might want to start thinking about a nice cosy office job at this stage.

Then of course there are the fears that every footballer has, whether he plays for Juventus or Oldham Athletic. These fears include things like injuries. No matter how fit you are, no matter how much you take care of yourself, every footballer at some stage is going to get an injury – and hopefully only a minor one.

Then there's the worry about being dropped from the team. After spending years working your way up through the ranks to the senior side, you may be forgiven for thinking that all the hard work has been done, that you can relax and enjoy playing in front of packed stadiums every week. Well, not quite. Every player, at some stage in their career, for whatever reason, has a dip in form. Usually, it doesn't last long, and before you know it you'll be back to your best. But while it lasts, it's not that nice and it can mean a spell back in...

The reserves. This is as far away from that sun-kissed World Cup moment of your dreams as you can get. A team's reserve side is an odd collection of up-and-coming young stars, old has-beens and players returning from injury and/or a bad run of form. All these players are trying to impress the manager enough to win (back) a place in the first team, and all of them are usually doing it in a near-empty ground with about as much atmosphere as the moon.

And finally there's the fact that, no matter which way you look at it, the career of a professional footballer is a short one. Germany's Lothar Matthaus may have (just about) kept going until he was forty but, usually, anyone over the age of 35 is reckoned to be over the hill.

We'll have some ideas on what may lie in wait for you after your glorious footballing career is over, as well as info on the other items mentioned above. But, if we haven't put you off completely, let's take a look at whether or not you've got what it takes to become a real pro, starting with possibly the most crucial aspect: attitude.

Who Do You Think You Are?

You may be faster than Ryan Giggs, more skilful than Dennis Bergkamp and have lovelier hair than David Ginola, but all that won't count for much if you're missing that one vital ingredient: attitude. Are you the type of player who just knuckles down, puts in lots of hard work during the week and delivers a highly professional performance come matchday, or are you more likely to turn up late (if at all) for training, ignore your team-mates and whinge when the manager asks you to at least try running after the ball? There's only one way to find out: imagine yourself in the boots of a top pro and take our simple test...

1 At your club, are you:

a) the captain, an inspiration to all those around you?

b) a quiet but hard-working midfielder whose efforts are greatly appreciated by your team-mates?

c) the nutter who spends most of the season suspended because of your poor discipline?

d) the one who organises all the parties?

2 You make a bad tackle on an opponent and the ref decides to show you a yellow card. Do you:

a) apologise to the ref and help your opponent back on his feet?

b) politely ask the ref why he has booked you?

c) walk away from the incident, making sure you're out of hearing range before shouting a load of abuse at the ref?

d) barge up to the ref, scream abuse in his face, then push him flat on his back before leaving the pitch, making rude gestures to the fans as you do so?

3 You're having a bad run of form and the boss tells you you've been dropped for the next game. Do you:

a) put in double the effort in training in a bid to win your place back?

b) tell your boss you know you've not been playing well, but that you feel you should have been given a little longer to prove yourself?

c) jet off on a two week holiday to Cyprus without telling anyone and later claim you were suffering from "stress and exhaustion"?

d) decide to go on "strike" until you're given back your rightful place in the team, along with a hefty pay rise as compensation for the appalling way you've been treated?

4 During the match you see a team-mate making an excellent run towards the opposition's goal. Do you:

a) make a superb, defence-splitting pass that lands right into his path

b) play a less risky ball to a team-mate closer to you?

c) hoof it in his general direction, keeping your fingers crossed that it reaches him?

d) ignore him completely, and attempt to dribble the ball around at least four defenders before scoring the goal of the season – it will look good on the telly tonight at least.

5 You're substituted 15 minutes from the end. Do you:

a) accept the decision gracefully and wish your replacement the best of luck?

b) act surprised at first, but then accept the decision – after all, the manager *must* be doing it for the good of the team?

c) trudge off the pitch slowly with your head down and without acknowledging the fans, the manager or your replacement?

d) storm off the pitch, tear off your shirt and throw it at the bench, and go to the papers the next day saying you never want to play for the team again?

6   One of your team-mates has become involved in a bit of fisticuffs with an opponent. Do you:

a) calm the situation down by talking to both players quietly but firmly?

b) steer well clear of the situation – it's got nothing to do with you and you don't want to get involved.

c) rush over and drag your team-mate clear of the problem?

d) rush over (from at least fifty yards away), push your team-mate out of the way and start a full-scale scrap with the entire opposition team which eventually sees you getting sent off and your team docked six points?

7 Your goalkeeper has just dropped a cross and cost you a vital goal. Do you:

a) console him – after all, anyone can make mistakes.

b) tell him you're very disappointed, but the team will get over it?

c) shout at him and pin all the blame on him for your team's failure?

d) ignore him and refuse to talk to him ever again?

8 At the end of the day (Brian) how important are you in the team?

a) "I'm the star and it's *my* duty to help the other less experienced players".

b) "I'm not the star but I play an important role in the team".

c) "I'm the player the manager always picks on if things aren't going to plan".

d) "I'm so important that the team would collapse without me – and to prove it I'm going on strike (again)".

So how did you get on? Tot up your answers and see which of these descriptions matches you the best...

Mostly As

Not only are you a very talented player, but you are such a nice young man that you'd make Michael Owen look like a nasty piece of work in comparison. Gary Lineker would be proud of you.

Mostly Bs

What you lack in skill, you more than make up for with sheer hard work and determination. You won't go far wrong with that sort of attitude.

Mostly Cs

Hmmm, you seem to have a very high opinion of yourself despite the fact that you don't appear to have the skills to match. You also need to keep a lid on that nasty temper of yours, otherwise a career in the Kidderminster Harriers reserve team beckons.

Mostly Ds

You're not exactly a team player are you? You could be a very successful player if you weren't quite such a prima donna. Button your lip sonny, and get on with the game. Or, if you don't fancy that, Aston Villa might give you a chance....

Get in Position

OK, so you answered mostly As or Bs in our attitude quiz. You've got the right approach to the game, of that there can be no doubt. What is in question, though, is what position would best suit you.

There are 11 players in a football team, but not all of them are strikers. "Blimey," you're no doubt thinking, "not much gets past this lot." Well, it sounds obvious enough, but if you did a quick survey of what position people dream about playing in, then most would probably say "centre forward" or "striker". Or "lean, mean, ruthlessly efficient goal machine". Perhaps.

It goes back to our "scoring the winning goal in the World Cup" fantasy. Strikers nearly always claim all the glory. Everyone knows that it was Geoff Hurst who scored a hat-trick to help England win the World Cup in 1966. And most people, even if they're not football fans, have heard of Gary Lineker and Alan Shearer. Whereas winger Steve Guppy is perhaps not quite such a household name. Not only that, but scoring goals is a good way to impress girls. Or impressing boys if you happen to be a girl reading this and fancy yourself as the female Dion Dublin.

But not everyone can or indeed wants to be a centre forward. There are a variety of other places to fill and now might be a good time to start thinking about where you want to play. So here's our quick round-up of who does what in what position...

Goalkeeper:

The phrase "You don't have to be mad to work here, but it helps" might have been invented for goalkeepers. Anyone who wants to stand between two sticks while rock-hard footballs fly towards them at great speed as burly strikers attempt to cover you in stud marks has to be absolutely barking. You only have to look at the likes of certain Manchester United goalies for evidence of that. Another downside is that, no matter how many great saves you make in your career, you will always be remembered for that one time you tripped over your own bootlaces and let in a goal during a crucial Cup tie with Bolton Wanderers. You have been warned!

Centre-backs:

These come in two varieties. One is the big, tall,

angry-looking type whose idea of passing the ball involves hoofing it as far away from the pitch as possible. The other is the big, angry-looking one whose idea of passing the ball involves hoofing it as far away from the pitch as possible and who shouts a lot. If that sounds like you, and if you fancy being the next Tony Adams, then carving out a career in the heart of defence could well be the logical choice.

Full-backs:

There used to be a time when full-backs could get away with having limited skills, as long as they had the ability to break an opponent's leg with a vicious tackle if that opponent had the cheek to try to dribble the ball past them. Nowadays that's not always enough, and full-backs are often called "wing-backs" – meaning they have to leg it up and down the wings as fast as possible, helping out with attacking moves as well as having to defend. So being a bit nippy and willing to get really stuck in are the main requirements for this position. Manchester United's Phil and Gary Neville and Arsenal's Silvinho are good examples of attacking full-backs.

Midfielders:

Like centre-backs, there are two main types of midfielder, although unlike centre-backs, they can be quite different. The first type, often known as the "midfield general", is the hard-working, tough-tackling, barking out orders to all and sundry kind of player who is usually described as having a "great engine". The second type of midfielder is your more cultured footballer – ie one who can actually pass the ball, sometimes even to a team-mate – and can talk to other players without feeling the need to scream his head off. You may hear this second type being described as having great "vision" and a wonderful "footballing brain". Whatever that means.

Forwards:

Includes strikers as well as wingers. Strikers you know about already. Wingers, on the other hand, are a strange bunch. They can either be brilliant, dribbling around defenders as if the ball were stuck to their boot, and whipping in great crosses for the centre forwards to tap home, or you can hardly notice them at all. Because of where they play, stuck out at the side of the pitch, they can drift in and out of games to such an extent that sometimes you can't even remember if they were in the team or not.

But seriously, folks. Footballers, like normal people, are all completely different. What position you play in shouldn't matter that much as long as you enjoy playing the game. Indeed, you just have to read the life stories of many players to realise that, just because you start off dreaming of becoming a legendary striker, you may well end up being a great defender.

Look at ex-Man United goalie Peter Schmeichel. In his first game as a young lad, Peter actually played in an outfield position. That was until he flew in with some rather reckless tackles and his coach decided to put him in goal where he couldn't cause as much damage! From there, of course, Peter Schmeichel went on to be one of the finest goalkeepers the world has ever seen.

No, what really counts is practising your ball skills and just improving your all-round game. Oh, and a bit of luck along the way wouldn't go amiss either....

Getting Spotted

Unfortunately, this isn't a soccer skills manual. Nor do we make any claims to be a football coach (largely because this is a paperback book, and football coaches tend to be short fat men in shell suits). So, sadly, reading this tome is not going to turn  you into the next Joe Cole — that will actually require some physical effort on your part.

However, having already forked out the dosh (unless you're sneakily reading someone else's copy) the least we can do is try to help put you on the road to success – starting with how to get noticed in the first place. So get ready for the first in a very short series of quick-fire question and answer sessions as we attempt to resolve your queries.

So, how do I go about getting spotted by one of the big clubs?

Well, assuming you're already playing for your school team, you should also think about joining a local side. Most clubs, especially the bigger ones, have a large network of scouts who scour their local areas looking for young talent.
So, joining a local team is the ideal way to put yourself in the "shop window" as it were.

At what age should I think about joining the local team?

As young as they'll have you! It's not unusual for professional clubs to spot and take on people as young as seven or eight these days so the earlier you start the better.

What if I'm not spotted by a professional club straight away?

Don't worry. The most important thing at this stage is to enjoy your football. If you enjoy playing then you shouldn't have to think about your future career too much. Man United's brilliant defender Jaap Stam joined his local amateur side in Holland when he was just seven and played with them for 11 years before he was eventually spotted and offered a professional contract!

So, I've joined my local team and a scout comes down to a game and decides he likes the look of me. What happens then?

The chances are he'll approach you and your dad or mum or whoever takes you along to the match and ask if you fancy coming down to their training ground for a few trial sessions.

Blimey! So what will these trial sessions involve?

Nothing too strenuous, especially if you are only eight years old at the time. You certainly won't be playing matches on full-sized pitches – it's

more likely to involve practising ball skills and teaching you about such things as keeping possession. You may also play a few mini-games.

Cool. So if I score a hat-trick in one of these mini-games then they'll sign me up?

Er, not necessarily. What they're looking for at this stage is to see if you have the potential to develop good technical skills and if you've got a good attitude to the game – ie whether or not you enjoy playing as part of a team rather than just as an individual.

But assuming they like me, will I then be offered a whopping great contract on the spot?

Steady on! You may have shown them that you have the potential to develop into a good player, but you ain't exactly proved to them that you'll be David Beckham Mark II yet. That is going to take years and years of patient dedication and practice as you progress through the club's numerous youth teams. You'll have to wait a while before you get your hands on that first professional contract. And, of course, not everyone makes it that far.

All that sounds easy enough – join a local amateur

side, play a few games for them, get spotted by a scout for a professional club and the rest is history. Of course, things don't always work out quite so smoothly and, for whatever reason, it may be some time before you are spotted – if at all....

The Youth of Today

As we mentioned in the last chapter, if everything has gone according to plan then you'll be training with your new club and all will be looking bright and rosy. But doubtless you've still got a few questions that remain unanswered. Yes, we thought so. So, as if to disprove the theory that sequels are never as good as the original, here's part two of our fascinating question and answer session.

How often will I have to go along to my new club to train?

Obviously it varies from club to club, but you can expect to train twice a week with them. In the meantime, of course, you can keep playing matches for your old local club.

But when will I have to finish with my old club and start playing games for my new team?

Again it varies. Not so long ago, it used to be the case that you'd stick with the training at your new club until the age of around 12, but these days you may well start small matches (six or seven-a-side) from as young as nine years.

Nine years old? Sounds a bit harsh.

Maybe, but clubs are starting players earlier and earlier now so that's what you'll need to go along with if you want to progress in the game. And being coached from a young age certainly will make a big difference to your overall game.

Why's that then?

It helps to get into good habits and get your basic techniques right as early as possible. Clubs like Ajax (from Amsterdam in Holland) have been doing this for years and have produced some incredible players through their youth system (a certain Dennis Bergkamp for one). Now English clubs are finally starting to realise that this is the way to go.

Will I get any help from the club's top players?

Yup – with many clubs you'll often get one of the senior players coming out to train with the youngsters to give them advice and tips, and to help build their confidence.

But what about my school work? How will I fit that in with having to train twice a week?

Hmmm, tricky one that. Obviously, it will make it harder to concentrate on your school work especially as all you probably want to do is play football, football and more football. And when it comes to your final year at school and revising for and taking your GCSEs it can become very difficult to find time to fit everything in.

But the teachers at your school will hopefully understand your plight. It will certainly help if you have a good relationship with your headmaster – and if the manager of your youth team speaks to him, then chances are something can be sorted out so you can continue both your studies and your football training.

So it's important to stick at my education?

Definitely. We know that football is probably the number one thing in your life at the moment, but you still have to have a Plan B if things don't work out. It all goes back to what we were saying at the beginning of this book – many people dream about playing football for a living, but only a fraction of them actually go on to fulfil that dream. It's a sad fact of life, but you have to be prepared for the worst. And, if you've got a few qualifications behind you, then it will make the disappointment a lot easier to deal with.

So how do things go on from there?

You'll play with the club's various youth teams (there

are several different age levels) until the age of 16 when you'll usually sign up on a YTS (Youth Training Scheme) and then, providing you make the grade, it hopefully won't be too long before you're signing professional forms and making your debut for the first team....

Make or Break

Making your debut for the first team? Getting a bit ahead of ourselves aren't we? You've got to get through the two years of being a trainee before you even think of mixing it with the big boys.

Of course, if you're particularly good then you may not need to complete the entire stint as a trainee and you'll find yourself in the senior side before you know it. But, that aside, what can you expect during these fun-packed, exciting two years?

Hard work. And lots of it. You may have in your mind a nice little routine of kicking a football around for a few hours, followed by a spot of light training, followed by trotting off home for a nice lunch and putting your feet up in front of the TV for the rest of the day.

Well, there'll certainly be plenty of training and playing football, but you'll also be given lots of, er, nice little tasks to carry out. These include such delights as:

✓ cleaning the toilets

✓ cleaning the dressing room

✓ cleaning your manager's office (hugely enjoyable, especially when the gaffer decides to work late, meaning you can't actually get into his office until nine o'clock at night)

✓ cleaning senior players' boots (a particular favourite this one).

So, lots of cleaning then. Perhaps not quite what you had in mind when you dreamed of a life in football, but important nonetheless. Any questions?

Yes. How on earth is tidying up some smelly, sweaty dressing room going to improve my football skills?

Good question. Obviously it isn't, but it will prove to your coach that you have the right approach to life. If you strut around with the attitude that you're far too good a player to even think about scrubbing out the bogs, then take it from us that the gaffer will be far from impressed.

But why does the coach want to make my life a total misery?

He doesn't, this is just something that every youngster must go through. Even Dwight Yorke had to clean boots at some stage. We know that all you want to do is play football, but get stuck in and show the boss that you're prepared to work hard and do whatever it takes to get to the top. Remember, that the coach is your friend and wants you to succeed as much as you do yourself.

So, er, I won't be home in time for the lunchtime edition of Neighbours then?

Not quite. You may be able to get away with that kind of behaviour when you're a pro, but as a trainee you'll be lucky to get home by seven in the evening. By which time you'll be so exhausted you'll just want to go to bed. Who said being a footballer was a glamorous life?

But obviously I'll get paid loads of money for working so hard?

You may have read in magazines and newspapers

about the likes of Roy Keane earning a cool £50,000 a week, but your weekly salary is likely to be closer to £50. And that's being generous.

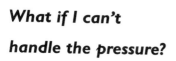

What if I can't handle the pressure?

This is the make or break stage for most players and not everyone can keep a cool head. After all, this is what you've dreamed of since you were a little kid and it all comes down to how well you do during these two years. If you're unlucky enough to get injured then you'll feel the strain even more. The most important thing is to work hard and keep a sense of humour about things.

And what happens if, after two years, the coach decides I'm not good enough?

Well, the first thing that happens is that you'll

probably feel very upset. No one likes being rejected. But just because you haven't made the big break at this stage, that doesn't necessarily mean your career in football is over. There are many players who have been knocked back at the age of 18 or 19 but have gone on to make it to the top.

Other players try their luck at a lower level with a smaller club. Some try their hand (or feet) at semi-professional and non-league football. Many stay in the game by carving out a career in one of the many other football-related jobs (see Chapter 12 for more details). And some decide that they want nothing more to do with the game and start out on a completely new and different career path.

And what happens if, fingers crossed, I am good enough?

Then you'll start training with the first team as soon as possible. And, yes, before long you'll be signing that first professional contract and earning large amounts of lovely cash. You'll still have to clean boots until the two years are up, though.

From there, you'll almost certainly have to go through a stint in the reserves. We talked about the strange world of reserve team football a bit in Chapter 2 and, if you impress the boss during these matches, it will hopefully be only a matter of time before you're making your first team debut.

Nervous? You will be. In fact, you probably won't remember much about the first few minutes of your debut, you'll be so petrified. Don't worry, it's only natural. But remember, if the gaffer didn't think you were good enough, he wouldn't risk his reputation by playing you. And, chances are, you'll get so swept along with the big stadium atmosphere that you'll soon forget about your nerves and start showing everyone what you can do.

And try not to be too disappointed if you don't immediately set the world alight with your silky skills.

Tales of footballers scoring hat-tricks on their debuts are few and far between. You're more likely to be thrown on for the last ten minutes of a rain-lashed cup tie away to Bury than you are to grab the glory and seal your place in the history books during your first taste of the big time.

All the Right Moves

We've talked about making your debut for the senior team. A thrill for any young player, certainly. But as many pros would agree, nothing can beat the incredible feeling of scoring, and your first ever goal for a club will no doubt become a treasured memory.

But before you go storming in, bombarding the opposition 'keeper with vicious swerving shots, you need to be prepared. Prepared for the possibility that you might actually score and, more importantly, prepared for the fact that you're going to have to celebrate in some form or another.

Let's face it, unless you've perfected a wacky dance routine to perform every time you hit the back of the net, you're not going to impress anyone. So, to help you out and give you some ideas we proudly present a sample of super soccer celebrations.

Celebrations come in two main types:

1 Team celebrations. As the name suggests, these celebrations involve the whole team. Because they require a bit of cooperation between all the players, they're often dreamed up and even practised on the training ground so everyone is well-drilled on how to celebrate come the big moment.

2 Individual celebrations. These can be much more spur-of-the-moment than team celebrations and can range from Alan Shearer's not-terribly-exciting "right hand raised towards the heavens" to a bewildering array of acrobatic mid-air stunts. More on which later.

TEAM CELEBRATIONS

LAID-BACK

Perhaps one of the laziest celebrations of all time came courtesy of Chelsea's Italian star, Roberto di Matteo. In his first game at Stamford Bridge, Roberto grabbed a late winner. He and his team-mates then proceeded to run over to the touchline and... er, sit down. OK, so they also each raised one finger of their right hands, but careful you don't overdo it, lads.

DAMBUSTERS

Another popular team celebration, this one (also known as the "running around the pitch with your arms outstretched pretending to be a plane" routine) was perfected by the Crazy Gang themselves, Wimbledon, way back in 1992 after a League Cup victory over Liverpool. Not that original, but at least more energetic than Chelsea's effort.

THE ROCK-THE-BABY

As first seen performed by Brazil at the 1994 World Cup and then ripped off by numerous other teams. So called because it involves pretending to "rock a baby" in your arms,

and is ideal for goal-scorers whose wives have just given birth. As indeed Brazilian striker Bebeto's wife had in '94.

QUACKERS!

Without doubt the strangest celebration ever

seen on any football
ground anywhere,
was invented by non-
league side Aylesbury
– also known as The
Ducks. The team
commemorated a
rare FA Cup win by
getting down on their

knees and waddling around like, yes you guessed it, ducks. Crazy stuff, but at least it got them a starring role on *Match of the Day* and *They Think It's All Over*.

INDIVIDUAL CELEBRATIONS

GUNNER

Playing for Arsenal makes any

striker's life easier when

it comes to choosing

a suitable celebration.

With a nickname

like The Gunners, the

obvious choice by a long shot

(sorry) to pretend your hand is a pistol and,

er, shoot it. As performed by Ian Wright and,

more recently, Nwankwo Kanu.

THE T-SHIRT

For players who want to get the message

across, the answer is simple: wear a t-shirt

underneath your club shirt with the message

on. When you score, whip off your club shirt

and your words of wisdom will be revealed to the whole football-loving world! Be careful though, because this can get you into trouble – as cheeky scouser Robbie Fowler found out when his t-shirt message showed his support for the striking Liverpool dockers.

EAR-CUPPING

This is the ultimate taking-the-mickey celebration. Especially useful if the opposition fans are giving you loads of stick, the idea is

to simply score a goal against your opponents then rush over to their supporters, cupping your ears in the face of the deafening silence coming from that side of the ground!

GYMNASTICS

If you're feeling particularly athletic, you might

want to consider some acrobatics. Players like

Robbie Keane and Peter Beagrie are fans of

these crazy celebrations which usually

involve jumping into the air and

performing a back-flip or

some kind of handstand.

Although they look

impressive, be careful –

you wouldn't want to

land on your head now,

would you?

It's Official

So you've made it. You're a professional footballer. You might or might not be playing for one of the bigger clubs but, whatever, you're earning a decent salary and you love your job. You're basically happy. At this stage, you might be forgiven for thinking that you can kick up your heels and finally begin to relax.

Well, we're sorry to have to shatter your illusions but nothing could be further from the truth. They may have been nice to you until now because you're young and fairly inexperienced, but there are a couple of forbidding looking figures on the horizon who from now on are going to be making your life very tough indeed.

Yes, you are going to have to deal with two of the most ferocious enemies known to man: managers and referees. There's no getting away from them. After all the manager is your boss and if you don't get along then there's no way your career is going to take off. And, given that refs control games – including who gets booked and sent off – then it's probably not a bad idea to stay on their good sides as well.

So without further ado, here's the lowdown on what makes these two strange species tick.

MANAGERS

[also known as: "boss" or "the gaffer"]

Although managers, like players, come in all manner of shapes and sizes they can be categorised into three basic varieties: Mr Tyrant, Mr Jewellery and Mr Eccentric.

Mr Tyrant

Nationality: Scottish

Appearance: dour, usually wears grey/black suit. Or a blazer if feeling in a particularly relaxed mood.

Habits: shouting, throwing cups of tea around dressing rooms, chewing gum non-stop.

Description: Mr Tyrant is without doubt the most frightening of all the types of gaffer. Not noted for his great sense of humour, his managerial skills involve terrorising his players into doing well. But although the team live in fear of being on the end of one of his dressing room dressing-downs, this also means that they'll do anything to avoid his wrath. Including winning every trophy in sight. For this reason, Mr Tyrant is probably the most successful type of manager.

Mr Jewellery

Appearance: large, balding, "comb-over" hairdo (see also Bobby Charlton), usually seen wearing a sheepskin coat and dripping in vast amounts of gold – rings, bracelets, watches and, of course, medallions.

Habits: buying jewellery. Lots of it.

Description: in the world of football, Mr Jewellery is somehow seen as a glamorous figure. This is almost entirely due to the fact that:

a) he wears a ridiculous amount of gold jewellery, and

b) he wears sunglasses – even in the winter.

Although he's probably the easiest of the three types to get along with, unfortunately Mr Jewellery's image is just that: an image, designed to cover up the fact that he has won little of note during his career despite having been in charge of a number of top clubs. Still, one thing's for sure: with Mr Jewellery around, life will never be dull.

Mr Eccentric

Appearance: scruffy, unshaven, windswept hair, often wears a shellsuit and, for some reason, a pair of wellingtons.

Habits: buying footwear which doesn't match the rest of his outfit.

Description: depending on how you look at it, Mr Eccentric is either a maverick – a tactical genius way ahead of his time, or such a complete nutcase that no-one understands a word of what he is saying. Which, when he's in charge of a bunch of footballers, is perhaps not a plus point. So, not the easiest gaffer to get along with. But, it's not all doom and gloom – chances are he'll be out of a job well before the end of the season.

REFEREES

Not quite as important as managers, but almost as strange, these men in black can make decisions that

appear mysterious so you'll need to get inside their minds to really understand why they are how they are.

The first thing you'll need to ask yourself is why on earth would anyone want to be a ref in the first place. With everyone from fans to players to managers to politicians hurling abuse at them, it's fair to say that they need to be pretty thick-skinned to stand the pressure.

So before you even think about hurling a load of abuse in the ref's direction, try and see things from their point of view. They are under a huge amount of pressure, especially these days with TV cameras covering their every move and mistake. It's pretty rare to hear anyone praising a ref if he's made a good decision, but if the ref has had a bad game, then everyone will want to have their say.

It's also incredibly hard sometimes for them to make the correct decision. Games are played at such breakneck speed that the ref only has a second to make up his mind, and his actions can change the whole outcome of the match. More and more players are cheating these days too, taking a tumble in the penalty area when they've barely been touched by an opponent.

All this goes to make the ref's job a lot harder.

So why would anyone want to be a ref? Well, the simple answer is that they're just like any other normal person – they love the game. Let's be honest, they have to if they're prepared to take all that stick week in week out! Contrary to popular belief, they don't set out at the start of the match hoping to send off a couple of players and book half a dozen more. Refs would much prefer to be in the background, barely noticed, allowing the game to flow for the enjoyment of the fans and players.

As top Premiership ref David Elleray says: "I enjoy being able to contribute something positive to a good game. If I've refereed well in a game that the players and the fans have enjoyed, then that's good too – no matter what the level."

And here ends the party
political broadcast on behalf
of the Referee Party.

Life at the Top

Fending off the attentions of refs and managers is just half the problem though. Once you're at the top, you'll also need to start thinking about your image – especially if you're playing in the Premiership and appearing regularly on TV highlights programmes. You're on the telly – therefore, you need to look really good.

And you're going to have plenty of time to think about it, too, because the average day in the life of a footballer isn't an endless routine of training sessions.

Of course, there is the small matter of actually playing matches, but these usually only happen once a week. And, of course, because you're playing that day you won't be doing lots of exhausting work-outs beforehand. Then you get Sunday off, unless you played really badly on the Saturday in which case the boss may decide to haul you in for yet another training session.

9 am:
arrive at training ground

10 am:
start training

12.30 pm:
finish training and have lunch

2 pm:
go home

And let's not forget that many footballers decide to do a lot of important, generous work for charity in their spare time. Which is all well and good, and we heartily recommend that you do the same. But for now let us turn to the other, some might say less important, matter of getting the right image.

CARS

It's absolutely vital to have (at least) one of these. For

a start, they're pretty useful for getting to the training ground. Fair enough, but they also have another function: they make you look very, very cool when you're behind the wheel of one.

Of course, your choice of car(s) depends on how much you earn as a footballer. But, for the sake of this book, let's imagine that you do play for one of the top clubs: Man United, Chelsea, Arsenal. Whichever one you prefer, you know you're going to have more money than you know what to do with.

So we suggest you start with a Ferrari. Or maybe a Lamborghini. Or, if you're a bit hard up, a simple Porsche Boxster should do the trick. The point is, it needs to be a sports car. A big one. Preferably red. German goal-scoring legend Jurgen Klinsmann used to drive around in an old Volkswagen Beetle,

pretending to be poor. But, frankly, that didn't fool anyone. You knew that, at the end of the day (or, more likely, at about two o'clock) he'd drive that battered Beetle back to a big house. A very big house. Probably in the country.

Heck, if you've got the money you might as well spend it. So a fleet of six top-of-the-range sports cars should be at the top of your shopping list. If you're feeling really rich, you may also want to hire your own personal chauffeur to drive you around. This means that, in each car, you can install TVs, drinks machines, PlayStations, music centres – anything you fancy as you're swished about town in your new toy. Marvellous.

MUSIC

Speaking of music centres, you're going to need to stock up on plenty of CDs to enjoy during your journey. The great thing about earning stacks of dough is that you can walk into any record store, grab a basket and proceed to fill it sky-high with as many albums as you like. Without having to worry about the cost.

The tastes of most footballers seem to revolve around the world of dance music and endless Ibiza compilations. Karaoke machines and singing along to old Elvis songs also seem to be great favourites. But if that isn't your bag, don't panic. What you listen to is completely your own choice. Just don't expect your fellow footballers to speak to you when you play the latest Steps CD on the team coach.

MOVIES

And speaking of the team coach, it's not just Cream in Ibiza Volume 82 that provides the in-journey entertainment. Videos, of course, will be just as important during your awayday travels.

Usually, one person is nominated to sort of out the film fun for these trips. If that turns out to be you, then you should be aware that no self-respecting footballer can be seen without the following vids:

a) any *Only Fools and Horses* comedy compilation

b) a selection of gangster flicks (*GoodFellas*, *The Godfather*, *Reservoir Dogs* etc)

c) one other comedy tape (you really can't go wrong with either a *Friends* or *The Simpsons* or *They Think It's All Over* collection).

IMPORTANT NOTE: We're joking, of course. There is no special rule book saying that all footballers have to listen to Ministry of Sound CDs and watch *The Untouchables* over and over again. Some, like Chelsea's Graeme Le Saux, enjoy such pastimes as collecting antiques and, would you believe, reading. Arsenal star Tony Adams, despite his hardman image, loves poetry and playing the piano. You may have to put up with a bit of stick from your Robert De Niro-worshipping team-mates but, believe us, that's their problem.

INTERVIEWS

And how do we know about all this stuff — how do we know what footballers do in their spare time, what they watch, what they listen to, what their favourite food is etc etc? It's because many of them are daft enough to give interviews to newspapers and magazines. Some of them were even so foolish as to speak to the writer of this book (after much begging and grovelling).

No doubt you've seen players being interviewed on the telly after the match. You've seen them answer such stupid questions as "So, you've just scored the winning goal in the last minute of extra time to clinch World Cup victory for your country.... How do you feel?"

What's more, they answer these questions without raising an eyebrow. Why? Because they're professional. Because speaking to the press is part of every player's life. Because, whether they like it or not, they're superstars, they're famous and people want to know all about them.

So, when a journalist asks you, for the umpteenth time, what "bangin' choonz" you like to listen to after training, just try to resist the urge to slap him around the face and neck. We're only doing our jobs, after all.

HAIRDOS

Far more fun than interviews, having an "unusual" haircut is a big part of being a professional footballer these days. Remember when David Beckham had his lovely locks shaved off? It made the front page headlines of some newspapers. That's how important hairdos are.

And if you want to get ahead in the world of football, then you'll have to give some thought to the style you're going to go for. A short-back-and-sides is fine for most players. It might also be fine for you. But if you want to stand out from the crowd, a little extra effort may be required. Luckily, the Spilling the Beans fashion adviser is on hand to answer any barnet-related problems you may have.

For a start, perms are definitely out. As are mullets (short at the front and sides, long at the back). These two styles may have been OK during the seventies and eighties, but then having a moustache was thought to be sophisticated in those days.

No, if you must have your hair long, then it needs to be long all over. The only problem this brings is that, like Patrik Berger, you may have to wear a slightly girly headband to keep your flowing mane out of your eyes.

On the other hand, if your hair is particularly thick and silky, you might be able to earn even more money doing the odd trendy shampoo ad. Like the lovely David Ginola.

However, the shorter the better seems to be very much the trend these days. There are a number of advantages to this:

a) you won't look like a girl

b) it may even make you look quite "hard" and "scary"

c) you won't need to wash it that often

d) it's easier to dye it blond. Which, again, is very important in these hair-centric times.

Of course, once you've chosen a hairstyle, there's no reason that you have to stick with it for the rest of your career. Look at Paul Gascoigne. The geordie maestro has been through a whole range of styles from the perm of his early days at Newcastle, to a mullet, to a bleached blond, and finally to the shaven-headed look of more recent years.

Cars, girls, money, rock and roll, and, um... hair. The world of football is indeed a glamorous and exciting one.
A shame, then, that it's usually all over before you know it....

They Think It's All Over...
It Is Now

Most people retire from their jobs when they're aged around 60-65. Footballers are a bit different. You may be lucky enough to break into the first team by the age of 16, although you're more likely to be closer to 20. By 28, most footballers reach the peak of their powers – young enough still to be quick and nimble, but mature enough to make the right decisions.

By the age of 30, though, you're considered to be "getting on a bit". By 34-35 you're "well past it". Anything over the age of 35 and you should really start asking yourself whether it's time to step down gracefully and let the youngsters have their chance.

Better diets and improved fitness regimes may mean you can squeeze a few more years of footballing out of your weary body. But there's little or no doubt that, in terms of career length, the life of a professional footballer is a short one.

Of course, you can still carry on playing into your late thirties, but this will almost certainly mean dropping down a division or two (or three) where your experience will hopefully make up for your lack of pace.

But say you decide to call it a day at the ripe old age

of 35. As we said before, most people retire when they're 65. What are you going to do when your career is over? Sitting around at home messing around on your PlayStation might be fun, but after 30 years of it, even you might start to get a little bored.

Although plenty of footballers decide, after years of playing, they've had enough and want to do something completely different, there are many others who choose to stay in the game they love and give something back to it....

COACHING

This is the obvious choice for many players. It allows you to keep fit and keep playing (practice games at least). More importantly, it means you can work with

other players —
from youngsters
right up to senior
pros — and it can
be very satisfying
to see them
progress and
improve with your
help. Having been a
player yourself
makes you pretty

much the ideal person for the job. For one, you will
have been through many of the highs and lows that
your "pupils" will go through — and so you can give
them the benefit of your great experience. Not only
that, but the very fact that you've already played at
the highest levels means instant respect from your
young hopefuls!

MANAGING

Unfortunately, the fact that you've been a decent

PERFORMANCE CHART

player does not always mean you'll be a great coach. And it certainly doesn't mean that you'll make a great gaffer. Football history is littered with players who flopped big time when they took the manager's hot seat. Bobby Charlton, a World Cup winner back in 1966 and one of the finest players England has ever produced, didn't exactly set the world alight when he took over the reigns at Preston North End. Alan Ball, another member of the World Cup-winning side, achieved the impressive feat of taking Manchester City – one of the biggest clubs in the country – down to Division Two.

On the other hand, some fairly ordinary players have gone on to be brilliant managers. The best example of this is, without doubt, Sir Alex Ferguson. The super

Scot had a pretty average career as a player at a number of clubs. As a gaffer, though, it's been a different story, with Fergie achieving great things at both Aberdeen and, of course, Manchester United.

In short: if you think you can handle the pressure, then being a manager is an exciting and rewarding job. But if you don't fancy being in the spotlight, perhaps coaching would be more up your street.

PUNDITRY

And if you don't fancy the stress of managing, or if the idea of putting on a tracksuit and running around in the freezing cold doesn't appeal any more, then perhaps a career in the media could be for you.

What could be simpler than turning up at a nice,

warm studio, watching a few matches on videotape, then chatting about them for a few minutes on telly in front of an adoring audience? Not only do you avoid all the hassles of being a manager, you also get to take home a decent wad of cash. Fantastic.

Of course, things aren't that simple (are they ever?). For a start, the number of jobs is limited, especially on TV — although there's always the chance of writing for newspapers and magazines. Secondly, you have to be the right sort of person. There's no point dreaming about being the next Alan Hansen if the minute you go in front of a camera you freeze up and can't say a word.

You need to be authoritative (know what you're talking about — or at least sound like you do), articulate (able to string more than two words together) and presentable (wear a nice suit). You also need to be prepared for the fact that many of your predictions will be completely wrong and you'll end up looking like a complete buffoon in front of millions of football fans.

And this is all assuming that you've already enjoyed a great career in football. But what if you haven't? What if you were one of the unlucky ones who were rejected at the age of 18? What if you were so awful that even Leyton Orient wouldn't give you a trial? What if, even after all that hurt and rejection, you were still determined to enjoy a career in this fantastic game of ours? The answer may well lie in the next, and indeed last, chapter of this book....

Behind the Scenes

And here it is, the last chapter. A sad moment, we know. But, hey, if you enjoyed the book, why not go back to the beginning and start all over again? Or tell all your friends to rush out and buy this fantastic volume. Just an idea. In the meantime, we've got to finish reading the flipping thing.

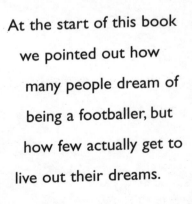

At the start of this book we pointed out how many people dream of being a footballer, but how few actually get to live out their dreams.

In this chapter we're going to take a quick look at some of the other jobs in the football industry. So, even if you have got two left feet, you may still have the chance to enjoy a job that you really love....

FOOTBALL COMMENTATOR

In Chapter 11 we talked about football pundits and how many ex-footballers go on to become pundits. The same is true of football commentators (Sky TV's Andy Gray for one). However, many

commentators have never played football in their lives (well, not at any serious level). It's a dream job which allows you to watch loads of football and get paid for it! Many commentators start off on local radio as a reporter and some move on to national radio and/or TV. If you fancy it, you'll need a good voice. Why not make a tape of yourself commentating and send it into your local station? You'll also need to be good at researching (background information on players which you can drop into your commentary) and have a good head for facts and figures!

MATCH REPORTER

Another great job which involves watching footie for a living. But although it might sound glamorous, it can take a lot of hard work before you're relaxing in the luxury of Old Trafford's press box being plied with free drink and food. You'll probably have to start off on a local paper as a junior reporter and work your way from there. Many colleges also run courses in journalism which will stand you in good stead. Other than that, excellent writing skills and a passion for your work are vital.

MATCH PHOTOGRAPHER

This job has many things in common with that of the match reporter – both the good sides and the bad. You'll have to turn up at the ground early and set your equipment up – choosing the end of the ground where you think the big "story" is most likely to happen. As well as sending your film off at the end of

the match, you'll also have to send a load off at half-time for the earlier editions of the papers. The pressure will be on to get a really good picture that you can sell, but if you're a bit snappy behind the lens then this could be the career for you.

WEBSITE EDITOR

In the Internet age, football websites have become a

massive part of supporters' lives. Working on a club website can be great fun as you'll get to know all the players, interviewing them on a regular basis. It can also be hard work as some of the bigger sites offer lots of different features like live on-screen "commentaries" on each match and on-line "chats" with star players! Although it's slightly more technical than writing for a newspaper, putting together a website actually isn't that difficult, so why not start up your own site as a hobby? It's the ideal way to find out if the work of a webmaster is for you.

GROUNDSMAN

As the name suggests, the groundsman is the man who looks after the ground. It's his job to make sure that the club's pitch is in tip-top shape for the whole season. And at bigger clubs the groundsman may also be responsible for the maintenance of the whole stadium. If watering a bit of grass sounds like an easy life, then think again daddio. The turf has to put up with a lot of wear and tear, so your work will really be cut out. You may even have to replace a whole

pitch mid-way through a season which could mean working round the clock to get it ready for the next home match. But come the big day, seeing the teams walk out onto that glorious green turf will bring a tear of satisfaction to your eye and it will all seem worthwhile.

SCOUT

We talked a bit about scouts in Chapter 5. They are, of course, the men who go round watching match after match after match, scouring the land for talent. You can either be a youth scout, meaning you'll be on the lookout for schoolboys who show promise.

Or you'll be on the prowl for older players who are already established in the game and will be able to slot into the first team quickly.

The long hours, and the thought of having to watch matches in the pouring rain or freezing snow may put some people off. But seeing a player that you picked up at a young age make his debut for the first team is extremely rewarding.

PHYSIO

Physios basically take care of the players' bodies, making sure they're in good shape and helping them with any injury problems they may have. As every club has its fair share of injury crises during each season, they are never short of work! If you fancy being a physio then you'll have to study hard (many colleges do courses in the subject with the chance to specialise in sports physiotherapy) but, like some of the other jobs mentioned here, working with the players is hugely satisfying.

And if you can't wait to get started on a career in football, you could try your hand at being a ball boy for a season. The job of the ball boy is to retrieve the ball when it goes out of play – as quickly as possible to keep the game flowing. Clubs choose their ball boys in different ways. At Arsenal, for example, they're selected from the junior members of the club. A total of 20 boys (and girls) are chosen and this select few are trained to catch and throw the ball accurately and to keep their eye on the game. Of course, it's great fun and you may even get the chance to meet your heroes.

These are just some of the many football-related jobs out there. Whichever one you think you might enjoy – physio, scout, reporter, or if you still fancy a crack at being a footballer – remember that the chance is always there for you to live out your dreams, in one way or another.

GOOD LUCK!